The Western Wilderness of North America

Photographs by H. W. Gleason

The
Western Wilderness
of North America

Photographs
by Herbert W. Gleason

Introduction & Commentary by GEORGE CROSSETTE

With a Foreword by STEWART L. UDALL · *Published by*

BARRE PUBLISHERS *at Barre, Massachusetts* · *1972*

The photographs by Herbert W. Gleason
have been printed from the collection of negatives
owned by Roland W. Robbins

CONTENTS

Foreword by Stewart L. Udall

IN the early years of the twentieth century only a few rugged souls, worthy of the title explorer rather than tourist, had actually penetrated the remaining wilderness areas of the North American Continent. Save for nature-mystics like John Muir, the only persons who explored the back country fastnesses were venturesome miners in search of a mother lode, the geologists and geographers of the government survey parties, and occasional big-game hunters in search of their prey.

Herbert Wendell Gleason took his first photograph in the last year of the nineteenth century. His professional subject was a parlor in a Minneapolis home. His photographic interests quickly shifted from the interiors of houses to New England's outdoors and eventually to his most ambitious project, the wilderness of western North America. Over several decades he climbed, hiked, and lived in the wilds, all the time making photographs having a quality and beauty equalling the work of today's finest photographers with their superior equipment. Gleason was an artist with the camera, and his work—only recently rediscovered—establishes him as an important figure in the history of American photography.

He also had other aims in his arduous search for breathtaking natural scenery. Fortunately for the country, Gleason was appointed an Interior Department "inspector," and one of his tasks was to photograph both lands included in the national park system and other areas proposed by conservationists as additions to the system. Many of his photographs lent strong support to the national park movement at a crucial point in its expansion.

Gleason was a fervent conservationist. One can guess that he had an intuition that as rugged as the wilderness areas were, they were still vulnerable to the incursions of modern man and his growing array of machines. Consequently, he wanted to preserve their unspoiled splendor on film. I believe he succeeded brilliantly in this effort. His photographs show each scene as it had been for millions of years, untouched by man. They are a timeless, invaluable record of the wild American landscape.

Adventuresome Americans today can stand where Gleason stood, and see what his camera eye recorded for the pages of this book. The national park system is a reality, and in large part the splendor which Gleason wanted to preserve has been saved. All Americans, especially those who visit the parks depicted in this book—Bryce, Zion, Yosemite, Yellowstone, Grand Canyon, Glacier, Kings Canyon, or those in British Columbia—should thank Gleason for this superb record of our outdoor heritage.

I commend both Barre Publishers and Dr. Crossette for their dedication to Herbert Wendell Gleason and his contribution to the history of conservation. They have snatched an important figure from near oblivion, given him his rightful place in Western history—and given us an invaluable chronicle of a time and place.

Herbert Wendell Gleason

SOMEWHAT over six feet tall, thin but well-built, Herbert Gleason wore a heavy mustache and retained a fine head of iron-gray hair well into his seventies. His manner was calm and quiet. His old friend Horace Albright, the second director of the National Park Service, called him "a gentle, kindly man."

Born in Malden, Massachusetts, on June 5, 1855, he was the son of Herbert Gleason of Plymouth and Elizabeth Upton of Malden. After attending the Malden public schools, he graduated from Williams College in 1877. The next two years he spent at Union Seminary, and in 1882 he became resident licentiate at Andover Seminary. He served as pastor of the Como Avenue Congregational Church in Minneapolis, Minnesota, from 1885 to 1888, having been ordained during this period. He was editor of the *Northwestern Congregationalist*, later known as *The Kingdom*, from 1888 to 1899.

In 1883 Gleason married his childhood sweetheart Lulie Rounds, who proudly traced her ancestry directly to Governor Bradford of Plymouth Colony. She was an accomplished pianist. They shared a full and happy life together, celebrating their golden wedding anniversary in December 1933. The fact that they had no children may help account for the scarcity of biographical material concerning Gleason's earlier years and religious vocation. Gleason died at the age of eighty-two on October 4, 1937, three years after his wife.

According to material Gleason supplied to *Who's Who in America* in 1930, he gave up his career as a minister in 1899 because of poor health. Thereafter, he devoted himself to photography and lecturing. He attempted some writing, including a 1915 book on John Muir entitled *Travels in Alaska*, but his principal interest was picture taking, wherein he showed a remarkable flair for composition and detail. Roland W. Robbins, of Lincoln, Massachusetts, who now owns a collection of some 6,000 of Gleason's glass plates, tells of the meticulous records he kept. They began with his very first photograph of the "Interior of Parlor and Hall, 1875 Columbus Avenue, Minneapolis, February 2, 1899." Thus, at forty-four years of age, Gleason embarked on his second career, one which is easily traced for the next thirty-eight years. His photographs and legends tell the story.

Gleason is perhaps best known for his pictures of Walden Pond and the Thoreau country, which he began to photograph in the fall of 1899. In 1906 he illustrated with his photographs the 20-volume Bradford Torrey edition of *The Writings of Henry David Thoreau* and succeeded in identifying a number of localities that were described and named by Thoreau but were unknown to any person living in Gleason's time. He made an excellent map of the Concord of Thoreau's day, showing the localities mentioned in Thoreau's Journal; this was first published in volume 20 of *The Writings* and has been reprinted many times. It contains many of Gleason's best photographs, along with nature commentary drawn from Thoreau's works. Even in this early work Gleason displayed exceptional attention to detail. The trait was noted by Professor

Walter Harding of the State University of New York who stated, "When Thoreau described, for example, wild pinks in flower near Heywood Peak, on May 30, 1854, Gleason returned to the exact spot at the end of May and photographed the descendents of those plants." Gleason's book entitled *Through the Year with Thoreau* appeared in 1917.

Gleason knew well the advantages of color in photography and surely prayed for a method which would permit him to make color transparencies. However, during his most productive years none of the early processes had been perfected. But this did not stop the Gleasons. To solve the problem, Mrs. Gleason became an expert at hand coloring the plates her husband used for lecture purposes. In a 1920 letter to Dr. Gilbert H. Grosvenor, President and Editor of the National Geographic Society, Gleason said, "The photograph of Rock Fringe really ought to be reproduced in color for it is one of the most brilliant rose pink alpine flowers I have found." He suggested to Dr. Grosvenor that the National Geographic Magazine publish a series of his flower photographs colored by Mrs. Gleason's expert hand. The combination of Gleason's photographic skill and his wife's excellent artistry led one authority to dub the pictures "the best of color lantern-slide collections."

While Gleason lectured for the National Geographic Society and wrote two articles for it ("On the Trail of a Horse Thief," April, 1919, and "Winter Rambles in Thoreau Country," February, 1920), his first pictures had been rejected by his good friend Dr. Grosvenor. As a purist, Gleason almost never permitted man or man-made objects to appear in his wilderness photographs. Dr. Grosvenor, on the other hand, had adopted the policy of having a person or thing in each illustration, as he explained, "to give some indication of size comparison." Stephen Mather, first director of the National Park Service, who in his eagerness to publicize wilderness areas had encouraged Gleason to submit photos to the National Geographic Society, was greatly disappointed. He said, "Oh, if only he had thrown his hat into the scene or even his knife or camera case." As a matter of fact, Director Mather had difficulty placing Gleason's pictures with other publishers for the same reason. To us today the requirement seems rather arbitrary.

Stephen Mather championed Gleason for many years and they became close friends. They had such faithful regard for each other that Mather, having been ill for some time while with the Park Service, decided to try the Boston doctor who had treated Mrs. Gleason after a stroke. The Gleasons often visited at Mather's Darien, Connecticut, home where the park director had turned a small stream into a lovely pond. One of Gleason's most beautiful photographs pictures Lake Stephen. The photographer was so moved by the scene that he wrote a poem, entitled "Lake Stephen," dedicated to Mather. An excerpt follows:

> . . . For once there dwelt
> Hard by thy shores a man of wise and loving deed,
> And thou wert his creation. A woodland brook
> That wound its way through sunken mead and fen
> He saw might be controlled . . .
> O lakelet dear, thy presence fair proclaims
> His noble character. Hence thy charm.

Mather appointed Gleason an Interior Department inspector, and it was at Mather's expense that the couple made many trips into the western wilderness areas. Gleason's duties were to take attractive pictures and observe conditions in general within the national parks and lands proposed for park status. Gleason and Mather agreed on the "purpose of the parks." They were not to be merely recreation centers for those who wanted only to play, but places to see untouched wilds, camp, hike, photograph, and in some areas hunt and fish. The photographs resulting from Gleason's work were used not only by Mather for his lectures but also by the Park Service and publishers to popularize the then little-known "wild West" and to promote the idea of national parks.

Using material gathered on his trips, Gleason himself gave lectures to publicize the parks and convey the need for further protection of natural areas. His western talks were very popular in the East and some 1,000 attended his review of "The Glories of the Sierras" at the Appalachian Mountain Club. One titled "The National Parks of America" was given in an eight-part series at the Tremont Temple in Boston.

During his travels Gleason must have spent weeks in railway cars and early automobiles. In 1919, he went with Mather, Grosvenor, and several others from Salt Lake City to the site of Bryce Canyon. Although the distance was only 270 miles, the roads were so poor that the trip took more than two days. This rigorous life seemed to agree with Gleason, however, and his health appeared to improve markedly after he began his photographic career. As early as 1905 he climbed Mount Rainier with a Sierra Club party, and in 1906 he tackled Mount Baker with the Mazama Club.

In addition to Mather, Grosvenor, and Albright, Gleason enjoyed the friendship of several other prominent people. He traveled extensively with Earl Grey, former Governor General of Canada. The photographer was also an intimate friend of Luther Burbank, and they worked together from time to time between 1909 and 1922. This relationship stimulated Gleason's botanical interests and he became a fine amateur scientist. He even included the Latin names of plants on his negative jackets and joined the Massachusetts Horticultural Society. His stationery carried the note, "Official Photographer for Boston's Arnold Arboretum." This was an outstanding honor since Harvard's huge botanical park is the largest living tree and shrub museum in the country.

Herbert Gleason became as active a naturalist-conservationist as existed at the turn of the century. He and his wife were supporters of conservation before the word had even come into popular usage. The couple's Christmas cards, usually reproducing examples of Gleason's magnificent photographs, often expressed their feelings. Their 1930 card read:

> In sending thus early to all our friends, East and West, our Christmas
> greetings and best wishes for a Happy New Year, we beg to make
> one request: Will you not, in planning your Christmas decorations,
> avoid using Mountain Laurel, Ground Pine, American Holly, and (in
> California) Toyon? Ruthless and commercial gathering has in many
> places practically exterminated these beautiful evergreens. Other

material, in large variety and equally decorative, can be secured, and some of it is surprisingly durable. For instance, a wreath of native Spruce kept its shape perfectly in our home for over three months. Yours, for the Conservation of Natural Beauty.

Gleason continued with his photography until less than a month before he died. His subjects spanned the nation. His coverage of Cape Cod was published in late 1971 by the Barre Publishers and is entitled *Thoreau's Cape Cod, with the early photographs of Herbert W. Gleason.* He made thirty trips to the West, covering Alaska, the Pacific Coast, the Grand Canyon, and the Rockies from northern Canada to Colorado. For thirty-eight years he explored the continent, recording and preserving for those to follow a pristine wilderness which he feared might be lost.

Little did Gleason then realize just how many were to follow. It has been claimed that tourists not only helped write the history of the West, but also, to a surprising degree, determined it. Traffic westward continued to increase from 1855, when Panama's trans-isthmus railroad opened, through 1869, the year in which the golden spike was driven connecting East and West by rail. By the 1880's the Pullman tourist was traveling in ever-increasing numbers. Many felt the West was never the same thereafter.

Yet, many of the wilderness areas destined to become national parks retained their original freshness. This would not have been true had it not been for men like Herbert Gleason whose mission was to attract sightseers to enjoy these settings but leave them as nearly as possible as they were when first discovered by man. He realized that America, being a young country, still had a chance to protect these natural gifts. He wished to avoid drastic changes such as those which have recently occurred in the 200-mile-long Glen Canyon, now Lake Powell.

In his crusade, Gleason's pictures became conservation tools as well as ornaments of beauty. The power and influence of a photograph must not be overlooked. It was the pictures of William Henry Jackson, another western photographer, that succeeded in influencing Congress to establish "Colter's Hell" as Yellowstone National Park.

Government land ownership is the first step in preservation, and it is fortunate today that a large part of the West is federally owned. In Nevada, for example, 87 percent of the state is public domain. A signal success of the conservationists was the passage of the Wilderness Act of 1964, which set aside millions of acres as protected lands and also provided for a program to study other areas for similar classification.

Great proponents of conservation such as Mather, Albright, and Gleason thought of parks as banks to store and preserve a portion of the wilderness. They sought to retain unusual natural features, not only to preserve the flora and fauna, but also to save a place where a man could stand in a wild setting with an unspoiled past he could not have known and expect his children to be able to do the same.

1 · *Grand Canyon National Park · Arizona*

THE Grand Canyon of the Colorado is described as nature's finest monument to the combined forces of uplift and erosion. During much of its life the elevation of the Colorado River changed little as it cut into the earth forming this great chasm. However, as it sliced its way through the layers of rock, the earth rose until at times the cutting barely matched the uplift.

These earth-shaping processes resulted in a gash some 200 miles long, averaging 9 miles wide and 5,700 feet deep. Erosion continues its work at a rate of some 6½ inches every 1,000 years.

There is evidence that man inhabited caves in the area nearly 4,000 years ago. The Indians have been long-time residents, from the time of the occupation of the Tusayan Ruin of A.D. 1185 to the Hopi and Navajo reservations of today.

Animals and plants have also long made the canyon their home. During the Age of Mammals camels, horses, sloths, and mammoths could be found there. Though most of these creatures no longer exist, a variety of animal life can still be seen, and more than a thousand species of plants exist in the canyon. There is contrast not only between the life forms of the two rims but also at different elevations. For each 1,000-foot increase in elevation, the effect on climate is equivalent to moving 300 miles northward.

In 1869 Major John Wesley Powell became the first recorded white man to descend the river. He described the canyon as an open textbook of the geology of the land, going back to the hard black rock of the early Precambrian Age before any form of life appeared on earth. Some visitors still find it most exciting to see the canyon from a raft as it shoots the rapids. Others prefer a muleback ride down the Bright Angel Trail, after being assured that the nimble mules have not lost a rider in over 50 years of threading the narrow trails. South Rim is open to tourists all year, but the North Rim, averaging 1,200 feet higher, is closed in winter. Though only 9 miles separate the two rims, they are 214 miles apart by road.

As early as 1882, Benjamin Harrison, then a senator from Indiana, introduced a bill in Congress to make Grand Canyon a national park, but it failed of passage because a number of senators feared damage to economic interests. Congress did not establish the park until 1919, when Woodrow Wilson signed the act. Gleason's photographs, taken in 1907 and 1913, helped stimulate interest in the canyon. But perhaps the greatest plea for its protection was made by President Theodore Roosevelt after his visit in 1903 when he uttered the now famous words, "Do nothing to mar its grandeur. Keep it for your children, and your children's children and all who come after you as one great sight every American should see."

Gleason's tripod and other equipment lie on the table in this well-sheltered site he called "Louis Boucher's Dripping Springs Camp." Park officials believe it may have been one of the early mining camps, probably on Bright Angel Trail near the bottom of the canyon. (July 5, 1907)

Gleason's passion for photographing flowers found full expression on his
western trips, as this beautiful shot of a yucca flower attests. Pale green in color,
the yucca resembles a cactus, but actually it is a member of the lily family.
When rubbed in water, its roots produce a thick suds, often used by natives as
a soap substitute because it left the skin smooth and the hair soft and glossy.
(June 26, 1907)

This view down the Colorado from Mohair Point is a fine example of Gleason's photographic skill. It reveals the care he took in placing his camera, composing the picture, and determining the proper time and light settings. He then followed through with the technical ability to process chemically the exposed 5″ x 7″ glass plates. Even with today's lenses, fine-grain film, and modern know-how, photographers would find it difficult to duplicate in quality this superb shot taken 60 years ago. (May 14, 1913)

Downriver from the foot of Bright Angel Trail the Colorado twists along with its burden of 80,000 tons of sediment a day. Before the Glen Canyon Dam was built it carried about six times that amount. Now Lake Powell, behind the dam, captures about three-fourths of the sediment formerly dumped into Lake Mead. During the July and September floods of 1927, the Colorado carried its maximum load—27,600,000 tons of sediment a day. (May 11, 1913)

Here Herbert Gleason, facing his camera upstream from the foot of Bright Angel Trail, took one of his rare wilderness pictures that included people. The river has been given many names, but only the Spanish Rio Colorado, or Red River, has withstood the test of time. This name, inspired by the great amount of red and brown silt the river bears, was certainly appropriate. (May 11, 1913)

This gnarled old piñon tree on the South Rim may no longer stand, for
Gleason took its picture on July 4, 1907. The piñon, a two-leafed nut pine
found in scattered groves on dry foothills and mountain slopes, is often one of
the first trees to gain a foothold as forests creep into arid lands.

On the west side of Grandview Point the strata or layers of the rock can be plainly seen. Once deposited on the bottom of a sea, these sediments now band the walls of the canyon. The agents of erosion, constantly whittling on the rock's surface, create varied forms and patterns throughout the canyon. (May 15, 1913)

2 · *John Muir Trail* · *California*

WHEN John Muir first viewed the High Sierras in 1868, he declared, "I am hopelessly and forever a mountaineer." Today the spirit of this naturalist lives on in the 212-mile-long John Muir Trail, which stretches through the wilderness he loved. Starting from the upper end of Yosemite Valley, the path twists through Yosemite National Park, follows the Sierra Crest for some 40 miles, then enters Kings Canyon National Park, and finally ends in Sequoia National Park near the Summit of Mount Whitney, highest mountain in the United States south of Alaska.

The earliest trails throughout the Sierras were made by the Indians on hunting and trading expeditions. Mining prospectors improved some of these paths, but it was the sheepmen and cattlemen who were responsible for much of the Sierra trail system.

Unlike most of the routes, the John Muir Trail did not cross the mountains but ran parallel to the range. The highest point on the trail, 13,200-foot Forester Pass at the Sequoia-Kings Canyon boundary, is only 1,295 feet below the crest of Mount Whitney. The trail is now a part of the Pacific Crest Trail, which extends from Canada to Mexico.

Interest in a High Sierra trail began as early as 1892 when Theodore S. Solomons proposed the idea. Later he and Joseph LeConte, along with many members of the Sierra Club, explored the canyons, mountains, and passes of the area. In 1914 a committee was chosen to seek the help of the state in constructing the trail. When John Muir, then president of the Sierra Club, died, his name was given to the trail as a memorial tribute. The state legislature appropriated $10,000 to help finance the work. The state engineer, though he selected the route and administered the funds, wisely called upon the experienced U.S. Forest Service for cooperation in the actual construction of the trail. Then, some 40 years after the trail's initial conception, the National Park Service stepped in to help complete it.

The organizations that worked so hard to build this and similar trails have now called a halt to further expansion stating, "Years ago the High Sierra was almost wild enough to protect itself. It no longer is." The trail signs give evidence of this: "No grazing of stock," "Trail closed," "Firewood scarce," "Stay on trail." The thousands of visitors have begun to change the environment. The natural areas exist for all to share, yet they will remain only if people learn to look, listen, and enjoy, but not destroy.

Muir's name will surely endure for it has been given to a mountain, a wilderness preserve, a grove of sequoias, and this magnificent trail. Having been a forceful writer and conservationist, he is often quoted. Of the Sierra range he said, "Climb the mountains . . . and get their good tidings . . . Nature's peace will flow into you as sunshine flows into the trees."

Cliff Creek Canyon is a scenic side trip the hiker will not want to miss when on the Muir Trail. From this point a rugged hike leads through 11,600-foot Black Rock Pass. The view from the crest is ample reward for the long tough climb. Authorities agree that even experienced parties with pack animals should not try to cover the entire 212-mile trail on one trip because time would probably not permit side explorations such as this.
(July 15, 1919)

Bubbs Creek Canyon, a tributary of the South Fork Kings River in southern
Kings Canyon National Park, is one of the frequent lateral rails leading off
the Muir Trail. Canyons such as this are common in the western side of the
Sierras, but on the east the range, being an uplift along a fault line, drops off
sharply. (July 22, 1919)

3 · *Yosemite National Park · California*

THE Sierra Nevada gave birth to Yosemite a hundred–million years ago. For myriads of years the Merced River slowly worked away, cutting a deep canyon. Then mighty glaciers came to dig it even deeper and wider. The glaciers also helped create the valley's magnificent waterfalls by slicing great sections of earth from beneath innocent little streams and causing them to plunge breathtakingly down into the valley. Glaciers pushed debris to the lower end of the valley where it formed a dam, confining a lake several miles long. In time this lake, filling with silt, sand, and rock, became the present valley floor.

The Ahwahneechee Indians lived in the valley long before the white man discovered it. In 1848, a group called the Mariposa Battalion was sent into the area to seek revenge for Indian raids. The Indians were destroyed, but their name, U-za-ma-ti, was given to the valley. Attracted by tales of the beautiful land, tourist parties soon came. In 1864 President Abraham Lincoln signed the document making Yosemite the first state-administered public park. It became a national park in 1890.

Yosemite is often referred to as the park that has everything—peaceful meadows, glacial peaks, high waterfalls, giant sequoias, and fascinating plants and animals. Today, like some of the other national parks, Yosemite is becoming overcrowded with visitors. Each year more than 2,500,000 visitors come to enjoy the park's attractions. They may venture forth along the park's 200 miles of roads, including a 30-mile drive to Glacier Point, with its panoramic view of the High Sierra and the valley 3,300 feet below. Dominating the seven-square-mile valley is El Capitan, a 3,600-foot monolith. The hardier visitor may wish to try a few of the trails in the park's 700-mile network. Nature walks, hiking, and saddle trips afford a close-up view of the high back country. Naturalists may study five of the continent's life zones, each with its distinct community of animal and plant life, between the foothills at 2,000 feet above sea level and 13,114-foot Mount Lyell.

In 1903, President Theodore Roosevelt spent several days in the park with John Muir. After their first night of sleeping under the giant trees the President wrote, "It was like lying in a solemn cathedral, far vaster and more beautiful than any built by the hand of man."

A number of these "glacial domes" can be found in the park. The rock was left completely bare when ice sheets passed over it, and in many cases the surface was polished to a high luster. The Indians, intrigued by the features, referred to Tenaya Lake as Py-we-ak, "the lake of shining rocks." (July 13, 1911)

The outlet of Merced Lake becomes a raging torrent during the spring thaw. The half-mile-long lake, among the largest bordering the western Sierra slopes, is one of eight lakes within the park where boating is permitted. Campsites are available, and the lake side is a favorite spot of visitors. (July 8, 1909)

Gleason's composite photograph of Half Dome is said to be one of the finest
pictures ever taken in Yosemite. Made from Glacier Point, it shows Tenaya
Valley on the left, Half Dome and Merced Valley on the right. In Merced
Valley are 594-foot Nevada falls in the distance and 317-foot Vernal Falls in
the foreground. The panoramic view is truly magnificent. (July 11, 1907)

Spring cascades high in the "back-country" were favorite subjects of both
Gleason and the great naturalist-writer John Muir, who is often called the
"Father of Yosemite National Park." As soon as his ship docked in San Francisco
Muir headed for the open hills, walking most of the way, and spent ten days
exploring Yosemite. From his first glimpse, the beautiful valley became
foremost in his mind and heart. (July 13, 1911)

When this mirrorlike pond was photographed in 1911, few persons had been privileged to see such beauty. Stephen Mather, first director of the National Park Service, commissioned Gleason to photograph similar scenes for park-promotion programs. Mather used the pictures to convince Congress and the people that the wilderness areas should be saved. Newspapers, magazines, post cards, and calendars took his message into homes and offices throughout the land.

The smoothness of these surfaces, referred to as "glacial polish," was caused by the great ice masses as they moved over the Sierra Nevada. Though most of Yosemite's rock appears much the same to the casual observer, geologists list twelve different types of granite alone. Small cracks, filled with wind-blown soil, offer a foothold to stunted pines, which struggle against great odds to survive in this barren landscape. (July 13, 1911)

A pack train crosses the hardened snow of 10,700-foot Vogelsang Pass on the crest of Cathedral Range. The riders in shirt sleeves suggest that the day was warm despite the heavy snow. Even today the pass is crossed only by riders or skiers. No roads penetrate to this remote area, although it is merely 15 miles from park headquarters. (July 14, 1911)

Gleason climbed 9,926-foot Clouds Rest on July 31, 1907 to record this scene on film. Cathedral Range, with the park's highest peak, 13,114-foot Mount Lyell on the left, forms the backdrop for this dramatic panorama. The park's main trail follows Merced Valley on the right. Side branches take hikers even deeper into these mysterious wonderlands.

McClure's Cascade is one of many which sprays hikers along the Fletcher Creek Trail to Vogelsang Pass. During July and August a park ranger-naturalist leads parties over the circular trail, stopping at rugged but comfortable High Sierra camps overnight. These attractive shelters, spaced about 10 miles apart, offer beds and meals for weary adventurers. Such conveniences are a sharp contrast to the conditions in 1911, when Herbert Gleason tramped through this wilderness. (July 14, 1911)

A fine example of the architecture of 1909, this cottage in the Wawona area with its fountain and gingerbread trim looks like a country estate. Nearby, in the Mariposa Grove, one of the three major stands of giant sequoias, is the 3,000-year-old Grizzly Giant. The circumference of this mighty tree is more than 200 feet. The popular Tunnel Tree, which fell recently, is not far away. (August 9, 1909)

4 · *Kings Canyon National Park · California*

KINGS CANYON and Sequoia National Parks in California join each other end to end, combining to form a 65-mile-long area with a single administration. Established in 1890, Sequoia is by far the older of the two, as Kings Canyon did not become a national park until 1940. Although set aside primarily to protect 30 groves of sequoias, both parks contain a great deal of high country, culminating in 14,495-foot Mount Whitney, the highest mountain in the United States south of Alaska.

Kings Canyon National Park lies near the center of the 250-mile Sierra Nevada, which in Spanish means "snow-covered mountain range." The park's canyon, with a depth of 8,350 feet, is the deepest in the United States, the better-known Grand Canyon being only 5,700 feet deep. Cedar Grove is the center of activity for the park. A road twists past scenic canyons for some six miles. From its end point hikers may follow trails farther into the high country which makes up four-fifths of the two parks.

Sequoia's popular General Sherman tree stands near the Generals' Highway. This 272-foot giant is estimated to be 3,500 years old. Nearby General Grant, Sherman, and Robert E. Lee trees are all among the world's largest and give the roadway its name. Not far from Giant Forest Village is the temporary tree home of the first recorded visitor, Hale Tharp, who built a shelter inside this fallen tree in 1858.

There are two species of giant sequoia; those of the mountainous inland area (*Sequoia gigantea*) and its coastal relative (*Sequoia sempervirens*). The park variety is the largest in volume. The General Sherman tree is said to weigh 1,450 tons and contain 50,000 cubic feet of wood. It measures more than 100 feet in circumference, making it the largest living thing on earth. The coastal redwood, on the other hand, being taller and slimmer, holds the world's record for height. Both trees are the last survivors of a genus dating back into ancient geologic times.

A wealth of animal life makes its home among these silent monarchs. There are more deer in Sequoia than in any of the other western parks. Bears, mountain lions, coyotes, and marmots are also seen as well as some 170 kinds of birds. Hikers along the 212-mile John Muir Trail, which passes through both the parks, will be thrilled by the variety of creatures observed.

Mr. Muir, for whom the trail was named, once said of the mighty trees, "No doubt these trees would make good lumber after passing through a sawmill, and George Washington after passing through the hands of a French chef would have made good food."

The 9,146-foot Sphinx, one of the park's more prominent features, is seen at the southern end of Paradise Valley. Gleason made this picture before the extension of the road in the geographical center of the park. He never hesitated to penetrate the most difficult terrain in his determination to record the wilderness landscape. (September 9, 1907)

Peaceful South Fork flows westward past Grand Sentinel Mountain on the right and 11,165-foot Glacier Monument on the far left. The park boasts 800 miles of streams and more than 500 lakes, with rainbow and eastern brook trout awaiting hungry anglers. Stream banks are largely free from vegetation and conditions for fly fishing are excellent in late summer and early fall. (September 13, 1907)

Aiming his camera east through Kings Canyon toward 8,514-foot Grand Sentinel, Gleason captured a beautiful young sugar pine on film. Though outranked in height by the sequoia, the sugar pine often reaches 200 feet. Its cones, a few of which scatter the ground in the photograph, are 15 to 20 inches long. (September 13, 1907)

Kearsarge Pass, less than 15 miles from Mount Whitney, cuts through the heart of the High Sierra crest. Only the hardy venture into this vast region of unbroken wilderness. Today, as in Gleason's time, forays into the forbidding realm can be made only on foot or horseback. Photographs such as this are of great promotional value to park advocates because few people ever see these sights in person. (September 11, 1907)

5 · *Yellowstone National Park · Wyoming*

YELLOWSTONE'S geologic history is one involving great change, for the park once lay at the bottom of a vast inland sea. As the water receded, the earth gradually rose, with volcanic explosions and lava flows following this emergence. Great mountain ranges grew, only to be eroded by streams and rivers. Finally great glaciers spread over the area, carving the valleys and canyons that exist today.

This geologic wonderland of smoking mountains, boiling springs, geysers, and mud pots was studied for four weeks in 1870 by the 19 men of the Washburn-Langford-Doane Expedition. They decided on the spot that these treasures must be preserved for all to enjoy. As a result, Congress declared Yellowstone the Nation's first national park on March 1, 1872. The work of William H. Jackson, who preceded Gleason in the art of park promotion through photographs, was also instrumental in stirring Congress to turn "Colter's Hell" into a park.

Not only the Nation's oldest national park, Yellowstone is also the biggest. Its 3,400 square miles make it somewhat larger than Delaware and Rhode Island combined. Within this area lies a wealth of unusual natural features. The park has its own 1,200-foot grand canyon, a lake with more than 100 miles of shoreline at an elevation of 7,731 feet—the highest large body of water in the United States—and the most extensive display of thermal phenomena in the world.

Best known of all the geysers is Old Faithful, which spouts some 10,000 gallons of hot water more than 150 feet into the air every 61 to 67 minutes. Worthy of its name, in 100 years it has never failed to erupt. Although Old Faithful is the park's trademark, it is neither the largest nor the most powerful geyser found there. Such steam and geyser action results when cold surface waters seep downward, perhaps a mile or more into the earth, and meet vapors from superheated magmas. The waters then boil upward to emerge in the many forms visitors love to see.

Another unusual attraction is Yellowstone's petrified forest. In most such forests the trees are lying on the ground because they were carried off by streams and then buried in sediments in low-lying valleys for millions of years. At the park, however, the stone trees are standing upright in the same place as they were growing. Originally more than 100 kinds of trees and shrubs were represented in Yellowstone's 40 square miles of fossil forest, the largest known.

The most popular tour in the park is the 145-mile Grand Loop auto drive, which winds through many fascinating spots and twice crosses the Continental Divide. Along this road, the alert visitor may spot grizzly bears, elk, or bison as well as many of the smaller mammals and birds that live in this amazing park.

Iris Falls, on Bechler River, is just one of many lovely waterfalls awaiting hikers
along the remote Bechler Trail. The streams and swamps of this area attract
many waterfowl, including the sandhill crane and the rare trumpeter swan.
All of Yellowstone is a veritable paradise for nature lovers and bird watchers.
(July 18 or 19, 1921)

Fishing and Yellowstone are synonymous. The best fishing waters are hidden in the back country, where dry-fly trout streams, like this one at Can Falls, are made-to-order for the "compleat angler." The only game fish native to Yellowstone is the cutthroat, but introduced lake and brown trout are doing well. Although licenses are not required, fishermen are expected to observe park regulations. (July 19, 1921)

Yancey's farm, as it looked on July 17, 1906 on one of Gleason's early visits, lies peacefully in Pleasant Valley, not far from Roosevelt Lodge. In-holdings such as this were a common problem for park officials. In some cases, life tenures were given the owners, but, as money became available, the government preferred to buy the properties outright.

Most visitors, thinking of Yellowstone in terms of geysers, hot springs, and bears, are surprised to find the park has its own "grand canyon" containing a waterfall twice as high as Niagara. Yellowstone's canyon begins at Upper Falls, a short distance above the 308-foot Lower Falls. Breathtaking scenes like this one from Grand View Point can also be enjoyed from Artist, Lookout, and Inspiration Points. (September 3, 1917)

Oyster Spring, in the Upper Geyser Basin not far from Old Faithful, is one of a series of hot pools. Most of these brilliantly colored springs are a delicate blue-green. After the 1959 earthquake the water temperature dropped some 10°F. to about 158°F., and rust-colored algae began to grow along the edges of the pools. (August 6, 1905)

Cleopatra Terrace is one of a series of terraces comprising Mammoth Hot Springs, located near the northern entrance to the park. Paths lead into an unbelievable fairyland of intriguing shapes and colors. Deposits of minerals such as travertine, a form of calcium carbonate, build up to form the shelves and pools. The bright tints are caused by various minerals and forms of algae that grow in the hot waters. (August 1, 1921)

6 · *Grand Teton National Park · Wyoming*

JUST south of Yellowstone National Park a huge cluster of mountains some 40 miles long rises abruptly to form what has often been described as the Nation's most beautiful national park. Youngest of all the ranges in the Rocky Mountain chain, the Tetons are a mere 10 million years old and are still rising. Slides and volcanic movement of the surface occur frequently, posing problems for maintenance men and engineers. The range was thrust up directly over a long fault and as a result lacks foothills. The highest peak, 13,766-foot Grand Teton, stands guard above Jackson Hole, the term "hole" having been used by early pioneers to indicate a valley enclosed by mountains.

John Colter of Yellowstone fame was probably the first white man to visit the area, in 1806. Other traders, trappers, and explorers came, but it was not until the 1880's that homesteaders tried farming in the high valley, which proved to be too cold for most crops.

In spite of its agricultural limitations, the valley continued to draw visitors because of its natural beauty. Lakes mirrored the snow-capped mountains from almost any vantage point. Mountain trails offered artists and photographers a wealth of subjects that could not be found elsewhere.

Attracted by this lovely setting, John D. Rockefeller, Jr., came to the valley in 1926. Through his generosity more than 30,000 acres were set aside as a "sanctuary of nature" and given to the people of the United States. The national park was officially established in 1929, and in 1950, Congress added the Rockefeller gift to the park.

Today Grand Teton is part of a large western outdoor recreation area that also includes Yellowstone National Park and three national forests, Shoshone, Targhee, and Teton, which border the park on three sides. The hub of this vast domain is the town of Jackson, Wyoming, crossroads for fishermen, campers, hunters, and skiers. It retains its "old time" appearance with wooden boardwalks leading to western-type stores, restaurants, and saloons.

Near Jackson is the National Elk Refuge, where as many as 15,000 animals have been winter-fed in one season. Moose, the largest member of the deer family, bears, and mule deer may also be seen by the observant visitor, along with many of the smaller mammals and more than 200 species of birds.

With today's hectic pace it becomes easy to understand why so many people are seeking the solitude of parks like Grand Teton. Here they may sit alone in an awesome, silent world.

The mountains were first given their name by a French trapper who called them "les trois tetons," or "the three breasts." Those that followed picked up the name, and today the great peaks are known as Grand Teton, Middle Teton, and South Teton. (July 14, 1921)

The Snake River, bringing debris from swamplands above, scatters its burden along the shores of Jackson Lake. Gleason did not mention whether the log shanty in the center of his picture belonged there or was washed down with the surrounding logs and branches. In the distance Grand Teton looms as the second peak from the left. (July 14, 1921)

Shortly after the two tributaries of Pilgrim Creek enter the park they join and flow some five miles over a sandy and stony bed such as this to Jackson Lake. Looking across Pilgrim Creek from the fabulous Jackson Lake Lodge, one can see the Teton Range beautifully reflected in the park's largest lake. (July 15, 1921)

The farm and hunting camp of Ben Sheffield, one of Grand Teton National Park's greatest promoters, is seen here as it looked in 1917. The settlement later became the town of Moran, which was eventually moved several miles to the southeast. This elaborate establishment, just below the dam on the Snake River, was purchased by John D. Rockefeller, Jr., as part of his gift to the American people. Ben brought into the valley and operated the first gasoline launch in Jackson Hole. The present Jackson Lake Lodge is located just beyond the tops of these buildings. (September 1, 1917)

7 · *Zion National Park · Utah*

MOST canyons are the products of several agents such as wind, uplift, or glacial action, as well as water. But geologists give the Virgin River full credit for the carving of Zion's canyon. There are no uneven, broken layers of rock along either side of the canyon. The layers on one face correspond to those on the other. Over the years the sand-laden river had gradually ground its way deeper and deeper into the rock.

Even today the process continues. Because the canyon is so narrow and its sandstone walls so steep, the sides are constantly being undercut. This process causes landslides and even the fall of large rimrock formations. It is estimated that the Virgin carries away more than a million tons of rock debris each year. While normally the river is relatively small, rains can turn it into a torrent that may rise 25 feet in 15 minutes.

The earliest human inhabitants of Zion were the Basket Maker Indians of about A.D. 500. The later Anasczi and Fremont peoples left the area about A.D. 1200. It was not occupied again for hundreds of years until the Paiutes came. They called the land "Pah-roos," or "muddy, turbulent water." The first white men to visit the area were probably the group of Spanish padres attempting to establish an overland route from Santa Fe, New Mexico, to Monterey, California, in 1776. Fifty years later the region was explored by a party under the leadership of the famous fur trader Jedediah Smith. From 1858 until 1909, when Zion was set aside as a national monument, Mormons farmed in the valley. In 1871 and 1872 Major John Wesley Powell, first explorer of the Grand Canyon, studied the region. His photographer, who preceded Gleason, took the pictures that first called attention to Zion's unique features.

One of these attractions is the Great Arch of Zion, a natural bridge some 600 feet across and 400 feet high. A favorite photographic subject is Checkerboard Mesa, with its wrinkled surface. Perhaps best known is the Great White Throne, which rises 2,450 feet above the Virgin River at its base.

Today the wonders of the park can be enjoyed throughout the year. The maximum winter temperature is 60°F., and snowfall is usually light, lasting only a day or two. Illustrated evening talks and guided tours are offered. For hikers, trails with interesting and descriptive names such as Angels Landing, Watchman Viewpoint, Emerald Pool, and Weeping Rock lead to the park's varied delights.

Checkerboard Mesa near Zion's east entrance is one of the park's most popular features. Gleason was intrigued by this spot, and to this day photographers delight in recording the unusual wrinkles on film. Thin beds of sandstone form the horizontal lines and cracks in the stone along planes of weakness create the vertical markings. The resulting pattern gives the face of the rock a "checker" or "biscuit" appearance. (September 16, 1921)

In one of the water-worn alcoves far up Echo Canyon, Gleason allowed himself to be photographed. This event marked a rare exception to Gleason's strict rule—no man or man-made objects were ever to appear in his wilderness photographs. No roads reached into this canyon in 1921, and Gleason undoubtedly carried his bulky equipment for several miles. (September 24, 1921)

Zion's "hanging gardens" appear as darkened areas on the opposite canyon wall. These small pockets are especially beautiful in spring and summer when filled with columbine, cardinalflower, and shootingstar.

Below, on the valley floor, the moonflower may be found. This large, trumpet-shaped, white flower is so named because it opens in the evening and wilts under the morning sun. (September 17, 1921)

From the canyon floor, actually an extension of the great Mohave Desert, the visitor is struck with an aura of mystery and disbelief. How did the tiny Virgin River cut this valley down from the height of the distant mesa? How can such a variety of plant life survive in these harsh surroundings? Perhaps a clue can be found in the meaning of the name the Mormons gave the area—Zion, "the heavenly city of God." (September 19, 1921)

Viewed southward toward the West Temple from the canyon rim, the great valley resembles a huge relief map. It becomes immediately apparent what prompted Clarence E. Dutton, brilliant soldier-geologist, to declare, "Nothing can exceed the wonderful beauty of Zion.... There is an eloquence to its form which stirs the imagination with a singular power, and kindles in the mind a glowing response." (September 17, 1921)

Here visitors can follow the footprints of the large three-toed dinosaur and study its reptile cousins of today as well. The park offers a wide variety of both animal and plant life, showing sharp contrast from wall to wall. The side with a modest amount of moisture sparkles with wildflowers, while the sun-parched opposite wall boasts only a few scrub oaks, junipers, and an occasional piñon pine. (September 15, 1921)

8 · *Bryce Canyon National Park · Utah*

PROBABLY the finest visual display in America of erosion's unending work can be found in southern Utah in Bryce Canyon National Park. Here is an unsurpassed array of unique and brilliantly tinted rock formations. Yet, the canyon's delicately carved spires and pinnacles are but temporary features, constantly being reshaped by the elements of nature.

Herbert Gleason recognized the beauty of this ever-changing scenery and began photographing it in 1921, seven years before the area became a national park. Nearly side by side he found arid deserts and meadows, great colorful canyons, and snow-capped peaks.

The story of the canyon's origin can be read from the spectacular rocks themselves. The process began some 60 million years ago, in Eocene times, when colorful rock materials from the surrounding highlands were deposited here in a great lake bed. Internal pressures later raised and cracked the terrain, and then water, in its various forms, began the task of creating a new landscape.

The layers of rock vary in hardness, and when attacked by water, the softer material is carved away first, leaving the harder substances in bizarre shapes. Most of the magnificent coloring is caused by the presence or absence of various minerals in the rock. In some places a thin layer of red sediment is found coating lighter stone. This results from an unusual form of erosion in which the colored material, like the wax of a dripping candle slowly runs down the formation, stuccoing the surface as it accumulates.

The earliest known settlers in this fascinating region were Indians of the Desert Culture who lived there about A.D. 1000. These people learned farming from the nearby Pueblos, then vanished. Possibly the group was absorbed by the Pueblos. But an early legend has another explanation for their disappearance. The gods, displeased with these immoral folks, turned them into stone and today they are the rigid spires seen throughout the canyon. The Piute name "Unka-timpe-wa-wince-pock-ich" means "red rocks standing like men in a bowl-shaped canyon."

The first white visitors on record were Mormons. One of these, a Scotsman named Ebenezer Bryce, gave his name to the area and left the first written description of it—"A hell of a place to lose a cow."

Pointing his camera westward toward Point Sublime, Gleason recorded this striking scene from the canyon rim on September 1, 1921. Many Bryce areas, complete with gardens of stone trees and shrubs, resemble settings created by Walt Disney, rather than the forces of nature.

For the nature lover, the park offers a variety of flowers, including the Mariposa lily, blue flax, paintbrush, iris, and primrose. Juniper, piñon, and bristlecone pine trees can be seen on the rim. The bristlecone pine was recently found to be even older than the giant redwoods.

A view from Boat Mountain shows Summit Crest in the distance. Trees have to struggle for existence in this dry and rugged terrain. In fact, the piñon pine shown here is large for the area. This pine, found growing 5,000 to 8,000 feet above sea level, is one of the nut pines supplying nourishment for birds, other small animals, and man. Once a staple food of the Indians and Mexicans, today the nuts are roasted and sold as a delicacy. (September 6, 1921)

In all, 347,000 visitors were attracted to this colorful setting in 1970. The 56-square-mile park offers over 60 miles of hiking and riding trails. Tourists may stay at the park inn or at cottages from May 15 to October 12. Bryce's neighbors such as Zion, Grand Canyon, and Lake Powell serve as added incentives drawing people to the area. (September 7, 1921)

Actually a three-mile-long amphitheater and not a canyon, Bryce is filled with fantastic shapes caused by the actions of rain, frost, and wind.

On a spring day visitors can distinctly hear erosion at work. During a thaw it is a dramatic experience to listen to the sound of water, falling rock, and the shifting of sand and gravel in the never-ending processes that change the face of the land. (September 2, 1921)

Boat Mountain in southeast Bryce Canyon is part of a narrow 20-mile-long strip on the edge of the Paunsaugunt Plateau.

Geologists have determined that the canyon rim recedes about one-quarter of an inch each year. While erosion is constantly cutting away at the phantom rock formations too, only a layer the thickness of tissue paper is removed each year, and they are likely to stand for millenniums. (September 6, 1921)

The Castle Group looks like fortresses to some visitors, groups of people to others. The patterns and shadows shift constantly with the changing positions of the sun and passing clouds. These formations are carved from one of the high blocks of the Paunsaugunt Plateau. This plateau rose from an ancient lake bed and then broke in several places, exposing the many cake-like layers. (September 7, 1921)

Many of the trails passing through these canyon formations are so narrow they never see direct sunlight. However, the light bounces off their steep walls so effectively that Gleason was able to take photos without using artificial flash equipment.

The Canyon's brilliant coloration is generally caused by the presence of varying amounts of iron and manganese in the rock. Mrs. Gleason painstakingly reproduced these vivid hues by hand painting them on her husband's slides. (September 2, 1921)

9 · *Glacier National Park · Montana*

GLACIER National Park comprises some 1,600 square miles of bold mountain range, with the Continental Divide winding along the crest like a serpent. Sprinkled throughout are snow-laden peaks, glistening glaciers, swift-flowing streams, waterfalls, and more than 200 sparkling lakes. This rugged terrain is largely the work of Pleistocene glaciers, which cut, pushed, and gouged out as great a variety of formations as can be found anywhere.

A number of Indian tribes, especially those of the Plains group, knew the area for its fine hunting and fishing, as well as a refuge from the summer heat. Portions of the park may have been seen by the Lewis and Clark Expedition in 1806, but the first recorded visitor was a Canadian, Hugh Monroe, in 1846. In 1910 President Taft signed the bill creating Glacier National Park. The Canadian and United States portions of the park were united and named Waterton-Glacier International Peace Park in 1932. The park's trails, like its animals, show no concern for political boundaries and wander from one country to another.

More than 1,000 miles of such trails fan out from the various visitor centers, and park officials recommend "even a half-day hike to the peaceful solitude of the remote parts." Even in summer some trails pass over snowbanks, and welcome shelters are numerous.

The park is a haven for more than 1,000 plant and animal species. Flowers in brilliant colors follow the melting snow up the mountain slopes. Showiest of all is the beargrass, a misnamed member of the lily family. At the higher levels are found mountain goats, actually a type of antelope. Grouse explode underfoot while hawks and eagles soar overhead and a wealth of smaller birds make their presence known in song. No fishing license is needed in the park, and some 20 kinds of fishes will do their best to outwit the most skilled angler.

Going-to-the-Sun Road, the only one crossing the park, is an outstanding scenic wonder. Running from Lake McDonald to St. Mary Lake, it climbs above timberlines for some distance and crosses the Continental Divide through Logan Pass.

John Muir once said of the park, "Give a month at least to this precious reserve. The time will not be taken from the sum of your life. Instead of shortening it, it will indefinitely lengthen it and make you truly immortal."

Glacier National Park offers visitors a wide range of activities in a spellbinding setting of
pristine wilderness. Those seeking to escape the bustle of cities find opportunities for boating,
fishing, hiking, horseback riding, and climbing, as well as an unlimited field for nature study.
For the less energetic, there is a magnificent drive over the Continental Divide at 6,664-foot
Logan Pass. From this point, miles of scenic grandeur stretch in every direction.
(August 14, 1917)

Herbert Gleason left little information about this photograph, except that it was taken on one of Glacier's larger lakes. The power boat, carrying the American flag and a life boat, would indicate that as early as 1917, when the shot was made, tourists had invaded the lakes in large enough numbers to justify such a craft. Today boating is a common sight but is restricted to lakes reached by designated public roads. This is one indication of the effort that is being made to preserve the park's natural beauty.

Lake St. Mary, at 4,483 feet above sea level, lies at the base of Going-to-the-Sun Mountain, which towers another 5,121 feet above it. The peak is frequently shrouded in clouds and bears a topknot of snow most of the year. One of the steepest mountains in the park, it is often the target of hardy climbers willing to risk life and limb on its crumbling sides. The tents at lower left could be Gleason's camp. (August 7, 1917)

10 · *Mount Rainier National Park · Washington*

AMONG the youngest of national park formations geologically, Mount Rainier was created by a series of volcanic eruptions less than a million years ago. The last violent eruption occurred about the time of the birth of Christ, and steam activity today shows that the volcano is merely dormant, not dead.

This 14,410-foot mountain, the nation's fifth highest peak south of Alaska, is mantled by more than 40 glaciers. Carbon Glacier, the largest, is over six miles long. Most of the world's glaciers are known to be receding, yet those on Rainier are expanding. Moisture-laden clouds blown inland from the Pacific are cooled over Mount Rainier and the Cascades. The resulting condensation produces rain and snow to feed the massive glaciers. Rainier receives as much as 80 feet of snow each year.

The Indians called the mountain Tacoma. They hunted in the region, but frightened by the smoking, snow- and ice-covered mountain, refused to live on its slopes. The first white man to view the mountain was probably Captain George Vancouver of the British Royal Navy. He named it for a fellow navy officer, Rear Admiral Peter Rainier, who never saw the peak.

The park displays an abundance of plant and animal life. The heavy precipitation encourages the growth of some of the West's largest trees such as the Douglas fir and Sitka spruce. These create a cathedral-like atmosphere in the dark awesome forests. Some 50 species of mammals and more than 100 kinds of birds make the park their home. It is especially thrilling to catch a glimpse of a group of elusive mountain goats or spot a marmot or cougar.

Gleason first photographed the area in 1905, six years after it became a national park. Today's visitors can explore the park on 300 miles of self-guiding trails. The 90-mile-long Wonderland Trail completely encircles the mountain. In season, climbing is a popular pastime, and even a novice in good condition can reach the summit after careful guidance and instruction at the required climbing school. The Glacier's ice caves are an usual attraction. Those under Paradise Glacier are especially beautiful with their striking colors and glistening illumination.

On his 1917 visit to Mount Rainier, Herbert Gleason visited the northern slope near the present Sunrise Visitor Center. From there he rode to Burroughs Peak and posed astride his horse. The cairn behind Gleason is man's way of marking a summit or memorial without defacing the wilderness. (August 23, 1917)

High above Paradise Valley on Mount Rainier's southern slope, Gleason photographed a typical volcanic upthrust formation. Such jumbled masses of broken rock lack the stratified pattern typical of rocks in areas where rivers have cut through the earth to expose relatively even layers of sediment. Although the distant valley with its sparse foliage resembles a more conventionally formed landscape, it too is volcanic. (July 21, 1905)

Glacier Basin, nestled between Emmons and Inter Glaciers on Rainier's north slope, affords pasture for the party's horses. Above, at the 9,600-foot level, lies Camp Schurman where a shelter cabin now stands for hearty climbers. Though Gleason made this photograph more than 50 years ago, the scene is very much the same today. (August 22, 1917)

A Sierra Club party on its 1905 climb, well-armed with walking sticks, crosses the stream above Sluiskim Falls about a mile northeast of the Paradise Visitor Center. A fine example of the sharpness of Gleason's work, this photograph is so clear that it is possible to see even the shoe of the young lady crossing the stream. Gleason in July 25, 1905.

Amid snowslides and eroded slopes 39 stalwarts of the Sierra Club stretch out in professional single file on an excursion to climb Mount Rainier. The same mountain was chosen as a training site for the 1963 American Mount Everest Expedition. Showing clearly the great bulk of the mighty mountain, which covers one-fourth of the park's 380-square-mile area, this shot was taken by Gleason on July 25, 1905.

As the snow drifts recede in late spring, plume or western anemones spring up in great numbers. The heads mature rapidly and begin to open when stems are only one inch high. As they grow, they become feathery, suggesting the hair of a small child. The seeds, bearing long tails to support them on their wind-blown journey, are gathered and stored by marmots and other small animals. A member of the crowfoot family, the flower may be found from California to Alaska. (July 7, 1905)

11 · British Columbia

THE people of Canada's westernmost province often call it by its initials "B.C." and name many towns and landmarks for places "back home" in England. Three-quarters of the population are of British descent. The capital city of Victoria is said to be so English "it brings tea to your eyes."

The setting for this transplanted bit of England is larger than California, Washington, and Oregon combined. The province includes 285-mile-long Vancouver Island as well as Queen Charlotte Islands, the crest of an ancient submerged mountain range which shelters the famous Inside Passage, a waterway linking Seattle, Washington, and Skagway, Alaska. The contorted landscape is often referred to as a "sea of mountains," for it is composed of a series of ranges, from the Rockies in the east to the Coast Mountains in the west. Mount Fairweather, at 15,300 feet, is the province's highest point. Scattered beneath the rugged peaks are rushing rivers, green valleys, deep canyons, and broad plateaus. Such scenery must have warmed Gleason's heart, for this was his kind of country.

As early as 1858, gold brought settlers to the region. Early visitors to this lush country encountered a rich Indian culture. The fishermen along the coast were the most advanced. Others, helped by metal tools, also developed the unique art form of totempoles carved in images of supernatural beings. British Columbia was also an ideal home for the legendary Sasquatch or Big Foot or Abominable Snowman, subject of much searching and controversy.

The visitors of today are drawn by British Columbia's beauty. They seek the calming solitude and peace of nature to be found in its parks and recreational areas. Like many a tourist from the United States, Gleason too was lured across the border by this pristine wilderness.

Though Calgary lies within Alberta, it is the principal gateway from the east to British Columbia's western national parks—Yoho, Kootenay, and Glacier. Calgary, located on the Trans-Canada Highway, has grown considerably since Gleason's day. He probably never visualized the extensive stockyards, annual stampedes, colleges, art centers, zoo, aquarium, museum, and other attractions found there today. (July 3, 1905)

Herbert Gleason describes this formation as "The Beehive." His eye-catching photograph illustrates nature's processes of erosion at work, constantly carving away mountains and sending rock debris downward to level off the land. The futile attempt of these trees to hold back the advance is only temporary. (1905 or 1906)

Glaciers may be considered rivers in slow motion, their speed being measured in inches per day rather than miles per hour. They range in size from a few square yards to the 600,000-square-mile Greenland Ice Cap. These streams of ice, moving downward along a valley between mountain peaks, are among the most powerful erosional forces in nature in spite of their leisurely pace. (1905 or 1906)

Herbert Gleason's 1905-vintage mustache, sideburns, cap, jacket, and narrow pants would not attract a second glance today.

Gleason never lost his love of climbing, indicating a complete recovery after he left the clergy "for reasons of health." Here he is roped to a companion on a glacier of the Sir Donald Range in Glacier National Park. (1905 or 1906)

Canada's Glacier National Park rivals its namesake park in the United States for breathtaking scenery. Although its 520-square-mile area is only one-third that of the Glacier south of the border, its peaks are higher and its back country is even more remote. The lady on the left, holding the old Crown camera tripod, could well be Mrs. Gleason. Her companion is carrying a camera or plate case. (1905 or 1906)

British Columbia's vast forests are still relatively safe from the axe, primarily because the more remote wilderness areas have not been linked to any of the transportation networks. This is also true of the hundreds of lakes and ponds, such as little Annette shown here. Gleason undoubtedly felt that by capturing these scenes and making them available to those who might never see them otherwise, he could convey their value by their beauty alone and perhaps suggest the need for protection. (July 6, 1905)

Mount Sir Donald rises to an elevation of 10,800
feet near the Connaught Tunnel, the Canadian
Pacific's five-mile-long passage beneath glacier-
covered mountains. The large glacier on the
right was a favorite subject of Gleason's, and
he photographed it from many angles.
(September 1, 1906)

Large glaciers blanket the north slopes of the Sir Donald Range. "Tailings" from
a higher ice flow are neatly piled along the left "bank" as though placed there
by a giant machine. This view, from the Cascade Trail in Glacier National Park,
is typical of the magnificent scenery encountered in British Columbia.
(1905 or 1906)

Now part of Canada's Glacier National Park, this beautiful valley of the upper
Columbia River sheltered many prosperous farms, even as early as 1906. This
striking photograph is an excellent example of Gleason's flair for fine
composition. (September 13, 1906)

Here in Windermere Valley the mighty Columbia River begins its wayward journey to the sea. David Thompson, first explorer to see the river, in 1807, could not believe it was the Columbia because it flowed northward. He established a fur-trading post in the valley and later followed the contrary river to the Big Bend where it turns south. (September 14, 1906)

"The Upper Columbia Valley looking north from Swanzy Peak plainly shows
the separation of the Selkirks and the Rocky Mountains. This view was taken
from one of the higher foothills of the Rockies overlooking the Valley." The
above legend, written by Gleason himself, accompanied this photograph when
it appeared in the April 1919 *National Geographic Magazine*.
(September 13, 1906)

Massive Mount Temple, just outside British Columbia in Banff National Park, rises more than 11,600 feet above sea level. As can be seen from this picture, taken on July 6, 1905, the peak may be snow-covered at any season. Gleason stepped into his own photograph at this rugged site less than five miles from Banff's famous Lake Louise.

This ridge, just south of the town of Glacier in Glacier National Park, is called Asulkan. The same name, an Indian word meaning "wild goat," has been given to a glacier, a pass, and a peak. The ridge hosts a number of great icefields on both sides. On the east the Asulkan Glacier flows into the three- by five-mile Illecillewaet. The literature does not explain how the Indian term "illecillewaet" or "swift river" came to be applied to a slow-moving glacier. (1905 or 1906)

Gleason described two-mile-long Lake Maye in British Columbia as "a lovely sheet of water, pearly blue in color." Icebergs, like those in the foreground, drift into the lake after breaking off the mile-wide face of the glacier spilling down from the surrounding mountains. The dark blanket covering the glacier is an accumulation of layer upon layer of dirt and other debris left behind after repeated meltings. (July 28, 1912)

12 · Epilogue

TEMPTED by any beautiful setting, Herbert Gleason did not confine his photographic pursuits just to existing or proposed national parks. Many of his best shots were taken in national forests, national monuments, wildlife refuges, state parks, or the vast tracts of unclaimed wilderness. His aim was to capture images of the country's magnificent natural areas on film so that others could share his enjoyment and appreciation of them.

In carrying out his mission, Gleason traveled over great distances. He spent months on railway trains, bumped over gravel roads in early autos, drove wagons, rode horseback, and struck out afoot to cover countless miles of rugged terrain. Altogether he made 30 trips to the West, averaging more than five days' travel time each way.

On these expeditions, Gleason carried an unbelievable amount of equipment. Today's photographer can tuck a one-ounce 36-exposure spool of film into his pocket, but in Gleason's time, he would have found himself carrying seven pounds of 5 x 7 glass plates to take that many exposures. In addition, Gleason toted a heavy camera, tripod, and all his processing equipment, including chemicals, trays, tanks, and a light-proof bag or tent for loading film holders. Undaunted by this weighty handicap, he often sought the most remote and inaccessible places for his picture taking.

While Mrs. Gleason did not accompany her husband on every trip, many times she went along, helping with his bulky equipment and making notes to assist in coloring his slides. Both were well aware of the importance of color and did everything they could to promote its use in printed form. On several occasions they submitted their hand-colored pictures to the *National Geographic Magazine.*

The results of Gleason's wide-ranging and artistic efforts were put to good use by national park promoters and conservationists in their programs and lectures. Gleason himself gave many talks to audiences interested in learning more about the western wilderness areas and how to protect them. The work of this pioneer photographer can truly be said to have contributed greatly to the preservation and perpetuation of the nation's natural heritage.

Cedar Breaks, a huge natural coliseum in Utah whose rim averages more than 10,000 feet in elevation, was set aside as a national monument in 1933. One of the Nation's most striking natural areas, it has been described as "painted like the wheel of a gigantic circus wagon." Its cliffs, white to orange at the top, turn to a deep rose or coral at lower levels. Though 2,000 feet higher and more colorful than nearby Bryce Canyon, Cedar Breaks was cut from the same geological formation. (November 23, 1919)

California's San Jacinto Peak rises 10,804 feet above sea level just 65 miles from the Pacific Ocean and less than 40 miles from the Salton Sea, which is 325 feet below sea level. The Indians claim that a powerful demon named Tahquitz lives on its peak and when he walks through the canyons howling and wailing, bad weather comes. This striking shot was made from Inspiration Point on Mount Greyback. (June 14, 1911)

Because of its eternally snow-covered crest, the Indians called Mount Baker
Kulshan or "the Great White Watcher." Although volcanic and still releasing
occasional wisps of smoke, it boasts twelve major glaciers. Moisture-laden air
masses moving inland from the sea release their burden on the 10,778-foot
California mountain and feed its forbidding icefields. (August 6, 1906)

The 400-acre Armstrong Redwood Grove, not far from the private grove
belonging to San Francisco's famous Bohemian Club, is now a California state
park. Nearby Santa Rosa was the home of Luther Burbank, with whom Gleason
worked for many years. Burbank chose the area for its near perfect climate and
soil and produced what he called his "new flower and fruit creations" during
his long stay there. (September 25, 1913)

Heather Lake, not far from Reno, Nevada, caught Gleason's eye. The Pyramid Range, part of the Virginia Mountains, lies in the background. A few miles away, near Virginia City, the fabulous Comstock Lode, which proved to be one of the world's largest silver deposits, was discovered. Mark Twain lived in Virginia City for a time and portrayed the booming town in his well-known story "Roughing It." (August 20, 1907)

Cypress Point offers a commanding view of crescent-shaped Carmel Bay at Monterey, California. Along these cliffs the once widespread Monterey cypress makes its last stand between Cypress and Lobos Points. Robert Louis Stevenson, who once lived here, called the wraith-like trees "ghosts fleeing before the wind." (November 11, 1907)

The Western Wilderness of North America

Designed by Klaus Gemming, New Haven, Connecticut.
Text set by Finn Typographic Service, Inc., Stamford, Connecticut.
Printed by The Meriden Gravure Company, Meriden, Connecticut
from prints made especially for this book from H. W. Gleason's
glass negatives, generously provided by Roland Robbins.
Bound by A. Horowitz & Son, Clifton, New Jersey.

Barre Publishers · Barre, Massachusetts